Gilbert Ford's

# HOW THE COOKIE CRUMBLED

### The True (and Not-So-True) Stories of the Invention of the Chocolate Chip Cookie

Atheneum Books for Young Readers
New York    London    Toronto
Sydney    New Delhi

Ever wonder where these
round, crispy, chocolatey pieces
of perfection came from?

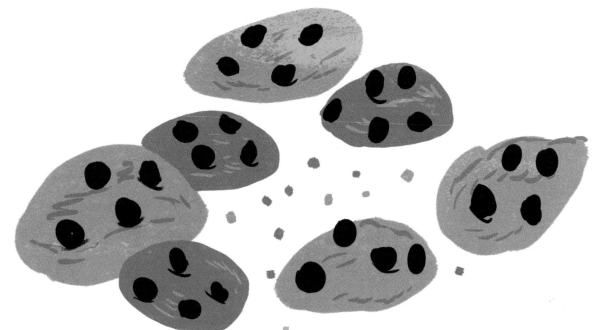

Everyone agrees that the chocolate chip cookie was
invented by Ruth Wakefield. But how did she do it?
That's where the story gets messy.
I'm here to show you some ways it could have
happened. So sit back, grab a cookie,
and let me sweep up the crumbs.

Ever since Ruth was old enough to hold a spoon, she was helping out her grandma in the kitchen. She'd carefully pour the scalding cheese into a rum-tum-diddy and measure with precision the flour in her applesauce cakes. You see, to Ruth, cooking was a science, and the kitchen was her lab.

So no one was surprised
when Ruth went off to college
to study nutrition.

After she finished school, Ruth went on to teach cooking in a high school. Although she enjoyed leading her classes, she hungered for something more.

Then Ruth met Kenneth Wakefield, who shared her passion for cooking. He quickly became the apple of her eye, and it wasn't long before they were married and cooking up a plan to run their own restaurant.

But their plan didn't fall into place until four years later. It was 1930—the beginning of the Great Depression—and with a young son in tow, it was not an ideal time to open a restaurant. But when our lovebirds found an old tollhouse in Whitman, Massachusetts, they knew it was now or never.

Ruth and Kenneth scraped up their savings, signed on the dotted line, and fixed the place up, naming it the Toll House Inn.

Ruth didn't let hard times stop her from opening her restaurant. She ran a tight ship, planning the menu and doing most of the cooking herself, while Kenneth ordered food and helped out in the kitchen.

Ruth's staff said she was one tough cookie to work for. She demanded that the servers set the tables flawlessly, and she even measured the distance between the fork and the plate for accuracy.

As diners began to trickle into the Toll House Inn, Ruth's hard work sure paid off. She sent her customers home with full stomachs and a craving to come back for more.

Now, here's the part where Ruth invents
the chocolate chip cookie.
The trouble is, no one can agree on how she did it!

Here are three ways the story has been told.

# THE DISASTER

As one tale goes, it all began when Ruth was whipping up a batch of Butter Drop Do cookies. Her mixer was spinning dough like a tornado, and it knocked a Nestlé chocolate bar off the shelf. The chocolate fell right into the mix and *wow!* What a disaster!

But the grill man suggested that Ruth bake the cookies,
anyway. Ruth gave it a try . . . and when she pulled those
cookies from the oven, she discovered pure heaven.

# THE SUBSTITUTE

Ruth was in a hurry. Our talented chef had forgotten to order baking chocolate, so she improvised by taking an ice pick to a Nestlé chocolate bar. She thought that by sprinkling the chunks into the dough, the chocolate would melt evenly.

But when she pulled the cookies from the oven, boy, was she wrong. "They're ruined!" she cried.

Of course, someone else in the kitchen took a bite and said, "Mmmmmm!"
When Ruth decided to try one herself, she agreed.

# THE MASTERMIND

While returning from a trip to Egypt, Ruth was pondering an old cookie recipe when inspiration struck her. Ruth got back to her kitchen and went straight to work, mixing up the dough.

Then she deliberately took an ice pick to that chocolate bar. Ruth dropped the chunks into the mix.

After the timer dinged, Ruth pulled the cookies from the oven and looked at her invention. It was exactly how she imagined it. She shut her eyes, took a bite, and savored the warm, gooey chocolate as it melted right in her mouth.

# So, which version do you believe?

## The Disaster

Although it is *possible* that the candy bar fell straight into the dough, this tale seems a little half-baked.

## The Substitute

Do you think that Ruth, who went to school and studied nutrition, didn't know how semisweet chocolate would melt when she cooked it?

That's a little hard to swallow.

**But here's some food for thought . . .**

## the Mastermind

Isn't it possible that Ruth actually knew what she was doing?

Anyone who knew Ruth would tell you she had a reputation for inventing delicious desserts at the Toll House Inn, and she traveled far and wide to find new recipes. If you ask me, Ruth deserves some credit. She was one smart cookie!

# Now, let's get back to the story.

Ruth placed the cookies on a platter, took a deep breath, and held them high. Then she marched into the dining room and presented her dessert to the customers. The diners pushed back their plates and reached for a cookie.

Word spread about Ruth's Toll House Chocolate Crunch Cookies, and folks drove from miles around to try one. So Ruth added more tables and expanded her restaurant.

People begged Ruth for her recipe, and she didn't mind sharing it one bit. She even sent it to the newspaper! Soon, everybody in Boston was baking Toll House Chocolate Crunch Cookies.

But it wasn't until Ruth was interviewed on the Betty Crocker radio show that word *really* spread. Now bakers all across the nation were talking about Ruth's cookies!

Meanwhile,
the managers at
the Nestlé headquarters
scratched their heads at the
spike in sales of their candy bars.

When they discovered that the cause was Ruth's chocolate crunch cookies, they begged for her recipe. Ruth gave it to them, and Nestlé began to produce chocolate chips designed specifically for Ruth's cookies.

And Ruth?

Legend has it she was awarded a lifetime supply of Nestlé chocolate!

By the 1940s every grocery store in America carried the Toll House cookie recipe on each bag of Nestlé chocolate chips.

From kitchen to kitchen across the country, cookies were baking.

After a long day in her kitchen, Ruth was able to sit and enjoy the sweet taste of success—in all of its crunchy, gooey, chocolatey perfection.

## Author's Note

**T**he chocolate chip cookie certainly put Ruth's Toll House Inn on the map, but Ruth didn't stop there. She went on to publish a bestselling cookbook, *Ruth Wakefield's Toll House Tried and True Recipes*. It contained all her dishes, including the ones her grandmother taught her. The book stayed in print for a long time.

Ruth's restaurant grew to sit one thousand people. Eleanor Roosevelt, Julia Child, Cole Porter, Joe DiMaggio, Bette Davis, and a young John F. Kennedy all stopped by the joint! The Toll House Inn sent American troops chocolate chip cookies during World War II so they could enjoy a taste of home while they were away fighting.

Ruth and Kenneth eventually retired in 1966, selling their Toll House Inn. The restaurant stayed open, selling Ruth's Toll House Chocolate Crunch Cookies until the establishment burned down in 1984. But Ruth's recipe didn't go up in smoke! In 1997, chocolate chip cookies were made the official state cookie of Massachusetts. Now, most people would consider the chocolate chip cookie a staple of the entire United States! It is arguably the nation's favorite cookie.

There are many tall tales claiming Ruth's chocolate chip cookie recipe was an accident, fabricated by kitchen helpers or even by Nestlé, who thought people would appreciate a story about dumb luck. However, in a later interview, Ruth said her invention was no accident.

# Toll House
# Chocolate Crunch Cookies

Make your own Toll House cookies using Ruth's original "recipe for success" from her *Ruth Wakefield's Toll House Tried and True Recipes* cookbook! Be sure to ask an adult for help when baking.

Cream 1 cup butter. Add:
  3/4 cup brown sugar
  3/4 cup white sugar
  2 eggs, beaten. Dissolve
  1 tsp. baking soda in
  1 tsp. hot water. Add
    alternately with
  2 1/4 cups flour sifted with
  1 tsp. salt. Add:
  1 cup chopped nuts
  2 packages of Nestlé's
    semisweet chocolate morsels,
Add:
  1 tsp. vanilla

Drop by half teaspoonfuls onto a greased cookie sheet. Bake in preheated oven, 375°F for 10 to 12 minutes. Makes 100 cookies.

To Mom,
who still sends me
chocolate chip cookies

## Bibliography

Bredeson, Carmen. *The Chocolate Chip Cookie Queen: Ruth Wakefield and Her Yummy Invention*. New York: Enslow Elementary, 2014.

Cooper, Kathleen. "Toll House Cookies: A Secret History." *The Toast*. December 5, 2014. the-toast .net/2014/12/05/toll-house-cookies-secret-history (accessed January 20, 2016).

Jones, Charlotte F. *Mistakes That Worked*. New York: Doubleday Books, 1991.

Leite, David. "Perfection? Hint: It's Warm and Has a Secret." *The New York Times*. July 9, 2008. nytimes .com/2008/07/09/dining/09chip.html?_r=0 (accessed January 20, 2016).

Thimmesh, Catherine. *Girls Think of Everything: Stories of Ingenious Inventions by Women*. Boston: Houghton Mifflin, 2000.

Wakefield, Ruth G. *Ruth Wakefield's Toll House Tried and True Recipes*. New York: M. Barrows & Co., 1948.

Wyman, Carolyn. *The Great American Chocolate Chip Cookie Book: Scrumptious Recipes & Fabled History From Toll House to Cookie Cake Pie*. Vermont: The Countryman Press, 2014.

———. "The Woman Who Invented the Chocolate Chip Cookie." *Slate*. March 20, 2014. slate.com/authors .carolyn_wyman.html (accessed January 20, 2016).

A special thanks to my fellow chefs, Emma Ledbetter and Lauren Rille,
who helped me bake up this story.

ATHENEUM BOOKS FOR YOUNG READERS • An imprint of Simon & Schuster Children's Publishing Division • 1230 Avenue of the Americas, New York, New York 10020 • Copyright © 2017 by Gilbert Ford • All rights reserved, including the right of reproduction in whole or in part in any form. • ATHENEUM BOOKS FOR YOUNG READERS is a registered trademark of Simon & Schuster, Inc. Atheneum logo is a trademark of Simon & Schuster, Inc. • For information about special discounts for bulk purchases, please contact Simon & Schuster Special Sales at 1-866-506-1949 or business@simonandschuster.com. • The Simon & Schuster Speakers Bureau can bring authors to your live event. For more information or to book an event, contact the Simon & Schuster Speakers Bureau at 1-866-248-3049 or visit our website at www.simonspeakers.com. • Jacket design by Lauren Rille and Gilbert Ford; interior design by Lauren Rille • The text for this book was set in Futura and Memphis. • The illustrations for this book were rendered in Doc Martin dyes, Adobe Illustrator, and Photoshop. • Manufactured in China • 0817 SCP • First Edition • 10 9 8 7 6 5 4 3 2 1 • Library of Congress Cataloging-in-Publication Data • Names: Ford, Gilbert, author. • Title: How the cookie crumbled : the true (and not-so-true) stories of the invention of the chocolate chip cookie / by Gilbert Ford. • Description: New York : Atheneum Books for Young Readers, [2017] • Audience: Age 4–8. • Audience: Grade K to grade 3. • Identifiers: LCCN 2016019687 • ISBN 9781481450676 (hardcover) • ISBN 9781481450683 (eBook) • Subjects: LCSH: Wakefield, Ruth Graves—Juvenile literature. • Chocolate chip cookies—History—Juvenile literature. • Cooks—United States—Biography—Juvenile literature. • Women cooks—United States—Biography—Juvenile literature. • Classification: LCC TX649.W33 F67 2017 • DDC 641.5092 [B]— dc23 • LC record available at https://lccn.loc.gov/2016019687